Countertop Inspirations

QUICK & EASY
FREEZABLE MEALS
120 TASTY RECIPES

BARBOUR

© 2010 by Barbour Publishing, Inc.

Compiled by MariLee Parrish.

ISBN 978-1-60260-899-3

Published by Barbour Publishing, Inc., P.O. Box 719,
Uhrichsville, Ohio 44683, www.barbourbooks.com

*Our mission is to publish and distribute inspirational products
offering exceptional value and biblical encouragement to the
masses.*

Member of the
Evangelical Christian
Publishers Association

Printed in China.

INSPIRATION
at your fingertips!

Looking for a way to simplify meal preparation? This book is for you. Within these pages, you'll find dozens of tasty recipes that are easy to prepare in advance, freeze, and are a delight to share with family and friends.

Finding a recipe is as easy as flipping through the book. Along the edge of each page, you'll see a color that corresponds to one of five categories:

So set this little book on your countertop, flip page after page for new culinary inspiration and kitchen tips and tricks, and you might just find a little encouragement for your soul in the process. Enjoy!

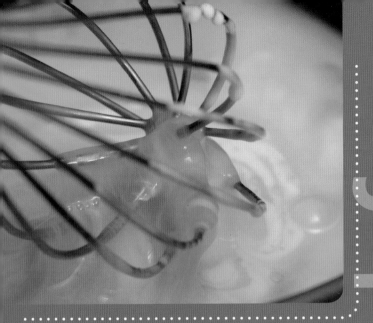

Breakfast Meals

Every good and perfect gift is from above, coming down from the Father of the heavenly lights, who does not change like shifting shadows.

JAMES 1:17

MEXICAN EGG CASSEROLE

1 small sweet onion, chopped
¼ cup green bell pepper, chopped
3 tablespoons butter
1½ cups corn
¼ cup black olives, sliced
8 eggs, beaten
1 cup sausage, cooked
1 cup sharp cheddar cheese, shredded

....

In large skillet, sauté onion and green pepper in butter until tender. Stir in corn, olives, and eggs. Add sausage and cheese, and cook until eggs are done. Pour into greased 9x13-inch dish and cool. Freeze 1 hour. Wrap in double layers of foil; label and store in freezer up to 1 month. To serve: Thaw completely in refrigerator, then heat in 300-degree oven for about 20 minutes. Serve with salsa.

CHOCOLATE CHIP GRANOLA MUFFINS

2 cups biscuit baking mix
1 cup granola
2 tablespoons honey
1 egg
⅔ cup milk
1 cup mini chocolate chips

Combine all ingredients in mixing bowl. Mix with wooden spoon until well blended. Fill greased muffin cups ⅔ full. Bake at 400 degrees for 15 to 20 minutes, or until a wooden pick inserted in center comes out clean. Freeze individually in sealed sandwich bags and then place in gallon-size freezer bags. Allow to thaw before serving.

SAUSAGE CASSEROLE

12 slices bread
3 tablespoons butter
2 pounds bulk sausage, browned and drained
2 cups sharp cheddar cheese, shredded
8 eggs
1 quart half-and-half
1 teaspoon salt
Dash pepper
1 teaspoon dry mustard

....

Remove crusts from bread. Butter 9x13-inch baking dish. Spread remaining butter evenly on 6 slices of bread and layer in pan with the buttered sides facing down. Top with sausage and then with cheese. Cover with remaining bread, buttered, with the buttered sides facing up. Combine remaining ingredients in bowl and mix well. Pour over the top of bread and cover. Refrigerate overnight. The next morning, bake at 350 degrees for 1 hour. Serve, or freeze for up to 2 months. If frozen, thaw completely before warming slowly in 300-degree oven.

SAUSAGE MUFFINS

4 cups biscuit baking mix
2 cups cornmeal
6 eggs
Dash pepper
3½ cups milk
2 pounds breakfast sausage, cooked and crumbled
3 cups cheddar cheese, shredded

....

Mix together biscuit mix, cornmeal, eggs, pepper, and milk. Add sausage and cheese; mix well. Line muffin pan with paper liners and spoon mixture into liners. Bake at 375 degrees for 12 minutes or until set. Allow to cool completely. Place each muffin in sandwich bag, seal, then place a dozen in large freezer bag. To serve: Microwave each frozen muffin on high about 90 seconds.

CHEESY HAM BREAKFAST MUFFINS

4 cups biscuit baking mix
2 cups cornmeal
6 eggs
3½ cups milk
3 cups sharp cheddar cheese, shredded
1 small onion, diced
1 small red bell pepper, diced fine
2 cups ham, cooked and diced

Mix together biscuit mix, cornmeal, eggs, and milk. Add remaining ingredients and mix well. Line muffin pan with paper liners and spoon mixture into liners. Bake at 375 degrees for 12 minutes or until set. Allow to cool completely. Place each muffin in sandwich bag, seal, and then place a dozen in large freezer bag. To serve: Microwave each frozen muffin on high about 90 seconds.

ERIC'S FAMOUS PANCAKES

3 eggs
1 cup milk
3 tablespoons olive oil
1½ cups flour
3 teaspoons baking powder
½ teaspoon salt
1½ tablespoons sugar
½ cup frozen blueberries

In mixing bowl, combine all ingredients except blueberries and mix well. Add blueberries and fold gently. Cook in greased frying pan, turning over after pancakes bubble. Allow to cool and place between sheets of wax paper. Freeze in freezer bags up to 3 months. To serve: Heat in toaster.

PUMPKIN CHOCOLATE CHIP MUFFINS

1 ½ cups granulated sugar
1 ½ cups light brown sugar
¾ cup plus 3 tablespoons canola oil
1 (15 ounce) can pumpkin puree
4 large eggs
3⅓ cups flour
2½ teaspoons baking soda
2 teaspoons salt
2 tablespoons cinnamon
1 teaspoon nutmeg
¼ teaspoon cloves
1 cup mini chocolate chips

. . . .

In mixing bowl, beat sugars with oil, pumpkin puree, and eggs until well blended. Combine flour, soda, salt, and spices in a bowl; stir into pumpkin mixture until well blended. Stir in chocolate chips. Fill greased muffin cups ¾ full. Bake at 350 degrees for 25 minutes or until firm. Freeze individually in sealed sandwich bags and then place in gallon-size freezer bags. Allow to thaw before serving.

HANDY CONVERSIONS

1 teaspoon = 5 milliliters
1 tablespoon = 15 milliliters
1 fluid ounce = 30 milliliters
1 cup = 250 milliliters
1 pint = 2 cups (or 16 fluid ounces)
1 quart = 4 cups (or 2 pints or 32 fluid ounces)
1 gallon = 16 cups (or 4 quarts)
1 peck = 8 quarts
1 bushel = 4 pecks
1 pound = 454 grams

Quick Chart

Fahrenheit	Celsius
250°–300°	121°–149°
300°–325°	149°–163°
325°–350°	163°–177°
375°	191°
400°– 425°	204°–218°

BLUEBERRY MUFFINS

1 ½ cups flour
½ cup sugar
1 tablespoon baking powder
½ teaspoon salt
1 egg, beaten
¼ teaspoon cinnamon
½ cup milk
¼ cup melted shortening, cooled
1 cup blueberries, fresh or frozen,
    rinsed and drained

....

Into mixing bowl, sift flour, sugar, baking powder, and salt. In separate bowl, whisk together egg, cinnamon, and milk. Stir egg mixture into the dry ingredients. Stir in cooled shortening until ingredients are just blended. Fold in blueberries. Spoon batter into greased muffin cups, filling each about ⅔ full. Bake at 400 degrees for 20 minutes or until golden brown. Freeze individually in sealed sandwich bags and then place in gallon-size freezer bags. Allow to thaw before serving.

BREAKFAST MUFFINS

2 cups flour
1 tablespoon baking powder
½ teaspoon salt
1 tablespoon sugar
4 slices bacon, cooked and crumbled
Bacon drippings left from pan
1 cup milk
2 eggs, well beaten

Grease muffin pan, and heat it in the oven while preparing the batter. Sift flour with baking powder, salt, and sugar. Fry bacon; put aside. Stir in bacon drippings, milk, and eggs. Add bacon. Mix until just blended. Spoon batter into hot muffin pan. Bake at 400 degrees for 20 minutes or until golden brown. Place each muffin in sandwich bag, seal, and then place a dozen in gallon-size freezer bag. To serve: Microwave each frozen muffin on high about 90 seconds.

EVERYTHING MUFFINS

BREAKFAST MEALS

2¼ cups wheat flour
1 cup sugar
1 tablespoon cinnamon
1 teaspoon baking soda
3 eggs
¾ cup applesauce
½ cup vegetable oil
1 tablespoon vanilla
1 cup carrots, shredded
1 apple, peeled and chunked
½ cup pineapple, chunked
¼ cup coconut, shredded
¼ cup pecans, chopped fine
½ cup raisins

....

In large bowl, combine flour, sugar, cinnamon, and baking soda. In separate bowl, mix together eggs, applesauce, oil, and vanilla. Add dry ingredients to wet ingredients and stir until just moistened. Stir in remaining ingredients. Spoon into greased muffin pans. Bake at 350 degrees for 20 minutes. Leave in pan to cool. Freeze individually in sealed sandwich bags and then place in gallon-size freezer bags. Allow to thaw before serving.

JAKE'S FRENCH TOAST STICKS

4 eggs, lightly beaten
2 teaspoons cinnamon
⅓ cup milk
2 teaspoons sugar
8 to 10 thick slices white bread

....

Whisk together eggs, cinnamon, milk, and sugar
in shallow dish. Dip both sides of bread into egg
mixture and cook in greased frying pan until each
side is brown. Cut each slice into 3 strips. Allow
to cool and place on cookie sheet; flash freeze
by allowing strips to freeze for about 30 minutes.
Then place in freezer bag and freeze up to 3
months. To serve: Warm in microwave for 1 to 2
minutes and dip in warm syrup.

BANANA CHOCOLATE CHIP MUFFINS

BREAKFAST MEALS

2 cups white flour
1 cup wheat flour
1 cup sugar
4 teaspoons baking powder
1 teaspoon cinnamon
1 teaspoon salt
2 cups milk
1 cup ripe bananas, mashed
½ cup butter, melted
2 eggs
1 cup chocolate chips

Mix dry ingredients. Make a well in center and add wet ingredients. Stir until just moistened. Stir in chocolate chips. Spoon into greased muffin pan, filling each cup about ¾ full. Bake at 400 degrees for 18 minutes or until golden brown. Cool 5 minutes in pan. Freeze individually in sealed sandwich bags and then place in gallon-size freezer bags. Allow to thaw before serving.

HERBED HAM OMELET

6 eggs, beaten, with salt and pepper to taste
2 cups ham, cooked and diced
1 tablespoon fresh basil, chopped
1 tablespoon olive oil
Butter

Combine eggs, chopped ham, and basil in bowl and blend. Cook egg mixture in oil for 2 to 3 minutes or until done. Butter a piece of foil and add the omelet. Cool completely. Wrap in another layer of foil; place in freezer bag and freeze up to 2 months. To serve: Place frozen omelet in buttered pan. Cover lightly with foil and reheat at 350 degrees for 25 minutes.

FRENCH & ENGLISH MUFFINS

3 eggs
¾ cup milk
1 tablespoon sugar
¼ teaspoon cinnamon
½ teaspoon vanilla
6 English muffins, split
Butter

. . . .

In mixing bowl, combine eggs, milk, sugar, cinnamon, and vanilla until well blended. Place muffins in large baking dish. Slowly pour egg mixture over muffins, turning to coat both sides. Let stand 5 minutes until all liquid is absorbed. Place each muffin in individual sandwich bag. Then place all muffins in large freezer bag and freeze up to 1 month. To serve: Remove desired number of frozen muffins and brush each side with butter. Place on greased, rimmed baking sheet and bake at 425 degrees for 10 minutes. Turn slices over. Bake 5 minutes longer or until golden. Serve with syrup.

QUICK QUICHE

1 refrigerated piecrust
½ cup sweet onion, chopped fine
5 slices bacon, cooked and crumbled
4 eggs
Salt and pepper to taste
½ cup sour cream
¼ cup milk
1 cup cheddar cheese, shredded

. . . .

Line piecrust with onion and bacon. In mixing
bowl, combine eggs, salt and pepper, sour cream,
and milk. Mix well. Pour over onions and bacon.
Bake in preheated 350-degree oven for 35
minutes, or until filling sets. Top with cheese and
cool completely. Place in large freezer bag and
freeze up to 2 months. To serve: Remove frozen
quiche from bag and heat in 350-degree oven for
35 minutes or until hot in center.

THAWING 101

Thaw frozen meat, poultry, seafood, or casseroles in the refrigerator 24 to 48 hours or until completely thawed. Foods thawed in the refrigerator can usually be safely refrozen without changing the taste or quality. For fast thawing, seal frozen food in a watertight plastic bag and cover with cold water. Change water every 30 minutes until food is completely thawed.

EGG & VEGGIE CUPCAKES

2 cups mushrooms, chopped
1 small sweet onion, chopped
3 tablespoons butter
2 cups broccoli florets
Salt and pepper to taste
10 eggs
1/8 teaspoon water
1 cup sharp cheddar cheese, shredded

Sauté mushrooms and onion in skillet with butter. Add broccoli and stir for 5 minutes over medium heat. Season with salt and pepper. Fill greased cupcake pans half full with mixture. In separate bowl, beat eggs with water. Add more salt and pepper to taste. Pour over vegetables in pans and sprinkle with cheese. Bake 10 minutes at 350 degrees. Place each cupcake in sandwich bag, seal, then place a dozen in large freezer bag. To serve: Microwave frozen cupcake on high for about 90 seconds.

BREAKFAST ROLL-UPS

BREAKFAST MEALS

1 tablespoon olive oil
½ small onion, chopped
2 cups frozen hash browns, thawed
8 eggs
Butter, salt, and pepper to taste
½ cup salsa
Whole-grain flour tortillas
Deli-sliced honey-baked ham
2 cups cheddar cheese, shredded

....

In skillet, combine olive oil, onion, and hash browns. Cook until potatoes are browned. Meanwhile, scramble eggs with butter, salt, and pepper. Add salsa. Warm tortillas in microwave 1 minute. Top each tortilla with 1 slice of ham and desired amount of potatoes and eggs. Top with sprinkle of cheese. Wrap in wax paper. Place each wrapped tortilla in freezer bag. To serve: Remove wax paper from wrap and microwave on medium-high for 1 to 2 minutes or until hot.

FRENCH TOAST

3 eggs
1 cup half-and-half
3 tablespoons sugar
1 teaspoon vanilla
8 thick slices french bread
1 cup cornflake cereal crumbs

....

Mix eggs, half-and-half, sugar, and vanilla in shallow bowl. Dip bread in egg mixture, leaving bread in bowl for a few seconds so it absorbs the mixture. Dip bread in cornflake crumbs to coat. Place on cookie sheet lined with wax paper. Freeze up to 1 month. To serve: Preheat oven to 425 degrees. Bake bread on greased cookie sheet 15 to 20 minutes or until golden brown and crunchy. Turn toast once during baking. Serve with maple syrup, jam, and powdered sugar.

CHEESY HASH BROWN BAKE

1 pound frozen hash browns, prepared according to package instructions
1 pound breakfast sausage, browned and drained
10 eggs, scrambled with butter, salt, and pepper to taste
2 cups sharp cheddar cheese, shredded

....

In buttered, freezable 9x13-inch baking dish, layer hash browns, sausage, scrambled eggs, and cheese. Cover tightly with foil and freeze up to 2 months. To serve: Thaw 1 hour. Then warm slowly in 350-degree oven until cheese is melted and center is heated, about 25 minutes.

BREAKFAST BURRITOS

1 pound pork sausage,
1 small onion, chopped
2 tablespoons butter
½ cup chunky salsa
12 eggs, scrambled with butter
Pepper to taste
24 flour tortillas, warmed
2 cups cheddar jack cheese

Brown sausage with onion; drain. In skillet melt butter; scramble eggs. Add salsa and eggs to sausage. Sprinkle with pepper. Mix gently. Place ½ cup egg and sausage mixture onto each tortilla and sprinkle with desired amount of cheese. Make burritos by folding in ends of tortilla and rolling up. Place on wax paper lined cookie sheets and freeze until solid. Then place individually in sandwich bags, seal, then in larger freezer bags. To serve: Wrap each burrito loosely in paper towel and heat in microwave on high for 2 to 3 minutes until hot in center.

SAUSAGE RICE BREAKFAST BAKE

1 pound sausage, browned and drained
2 (14 ounce) cans cream of celery soup
6 eggs, beaten
1 small onion, chopped fine
⅓ cup white rice (not instant)
6 cups crispy rice cereal
3 cups sharp cheddar cheese, shredded

....

In large bowl, combine all ingredients and mix well. Pour into greased 9x13-inch dish. Freeze up to 2 months. To serve: Thaw overnight in refrigerator. Bake covered at 375 degrees for 30 minutes. Uncover and bake another 45 minutes or until rice is done.

GOOD MORNING CASSEROLE

10 large eggs, beaten
2½ cups milk
1 teaspoon salt
1 teaspoon mustard
8 slices bread, cubed
1 cup sharp cheddar cheese, shredded
1 pound pork sausage, cooked and crumbled

....

In large bowl, combine eggs, milk, salt, and mustard. Stir in bread, cheese, and sausage. Mix thoroughly. Spread mixture into buttered 9x13-inch pan. Cover with foil and refrigerate at least 12 hours before baking. Bake at 350 degrees for 35 minutes. Allow to cool. Cut into large squares and place in individual sandwich bags. Then place in larger freezer bag. To serve: Microwave on high about 90 seconds or until hot.

VEGGIE BREAKFAST BAKE

4½ cups seasoned croutons
2 cups sharp cheddar cheese, shredded
1 medium sweet onion, chopped
¼ cup red bell pepper, chopped
¼ cup green bell pepper, chopped
1 (4½ ounce) jar sliced mushrooms, drained
8 eggs
4 cups milk
1 teaspoon salt
¼ teaspoon pepper
8 bacon strips, cooked and crumbled

....

Sprinkle croutons, cheese, onion, peppers, and mushrooms into 2 greased 8x8-inch baking dishes. In bowl, combine eggs, milk, salt, and pepper. Pour over vegetables and sprinkle with bacon. Cover tightly and freeze up to 3 months. To serve: Thaw in refrigerator overnight. Bring to room temperature about 1 hour and then bake uncovered at 350 degrees for 55 minutes or until knife comes out clean.

AVOID FREEZER BURN

Freezer burn happens when air comes in contact with food and pulls out all the moisture. Preventing freezer burn starts with proper storage of freezer foods. Remove as much air as possible from zippered freezer bags, invest in airtight freezable containers, and double-foil food whenever possible.

Quick Tip

ENGLISH MUFFIN BREAKFAST PIZZAS

1/4 cup butter, softened
2 1/2 ounces processed sharp cheddar
   cheese spread
1/2 pound pork sausage
1 onion, chopped and drained
12 English muffins, split

....

In large bowl, combine butter and cheese spread
and blend well. Cook sausage, with onions,
combine mixture with cheese mixture. Spread
mixture generously on split side of muffin halves.
Place on ungreased cookie sheet and bake at
350 degrees for 10 to 15 minutes. Cool and flash
freeze on cookie sheets by allowing pizzas to
freeze for about 30 minutes. Place in sandwich
bags, seal, then place in heavy-duty freezer bags. To
serve: Microwave each pizza for 1 to 2 minutes on
high until pizzas are hot and cheese is melted.

Lunches

Love must be sincere. Hate what is evil;
cling to what is good.

ROMANS 12:9

FRENCH DIP SANDWICHES

4 large french rolls
2 tablespoons butter
½ pound deli roast beef
4 slices provolone cheese

....

Split rolls and spread with butter. Top with beef
and cheese and fold rolls over. Wrap in aluminum
foil and store in freezer bag up to 2 weeks.
To serve: Remove foil and reheat in oven or
microwave until warm. Serve with your favorite au
jus dipping sauce.

HEALTHY PIZZA BAGELS

12 large whole-wheat bagels
Pizza sauce
Turkey pepperoni
Mozzarella cheese

....

Cut bagels in half and place them faceup on
workspace. Spread pizza sauce in thin layer
on each half, then add
toppings. Sprinkle with
cheese and broil in oven
until cheese melts. Cool
completely, then package
them individually (half a
bagel per bag). Freeze. Can
be put into school lunches
frozen, and they will thaw
by lunchtime.

HORSEY SANDWICHES

4 ounces cream cheese, softened
1 tablespoon horseradish
1 loaf rye bread, sliced
1 pound deli roast beef

In mixing bowl, blend cream cheese and horseradish. Spread mixture evenly onto each slice of bread. Add roast beef to half the slices and top with another slice of bread. Wrap sandwiches in foil and place in large freezer bag. Freeze up to 2 weeks. To serve: Remove from freezer in the morning and it will be thawed by lunchtime.

TUNA SANDWICHES

12 teaspoons butter
12 slices whole-wheat bread
3 ounces cream cheese, softened
1 tablespoon lemon juice
1 tablespoon sweet relish
2 (6 ounce) cans tuna, drained and flaked

Butter 2 slices of bread for each sandwich. In mixing bowl, blend cream cheese, lemon juice, and relish. Add tuna and mix well. Spread mixture onto buttered side of 6 slices of bread. Top each with another slice of bread, buttered side down. Wrap in foil and place in a large freezer bag. Freeze for up to 2 weeks. To serve: Remove from freezer in the morning and it will be thawed by lunchtime.

SLOPPY JOES

2 pounds lean ground beef
1 medium onion, chopped
¾ cup brown sugar
1 tablespoon mustard
½ cup ketchup
2 tablespoons prepared barbecue sauce
Buns

. . . .

Brown ground beef and onion in large skillet.
Drain. Add remaining ingredients and simmer 5
minutes. Allow to cool and place in freezer-safe
storage container. Freeze up to 3 months. To
serve: Warm in microwave on medium-high for 5
minutes or until hot. Serve on buns.

CHICKEN QUESADILLAS

2 pounds boneless, skinless chicken breast,
   cooked and shredded
1 (4 ounce) can diced green chilies
1 pound cheddar jack cheese, shredded
1 dozen flour tortillas
3 tablespoons butter

· ·

In large bowl, mix chicken, chilies, and cheese.
Freeze in freezable storage container up to 3
months. You may also freeze the tortillas. To serve:
Allow chicken to thaw overnight in refrigerator.
Butter one side of each tortilla. Spoon mixture
onto one tortilla, with buttered side down, cover
with a second tortilla, buttered side up, and
lightly brown on each side in greased skillet over
medium-high heat.

LUNCHES

ITALIAN-STYLE FREEZER SANDWICHES

1 pound ground turkey breast,
  browned and drained
½ cup onion, chopped
1 (4 ounce) can diced green chilies
1 (15 ounce) can tomato sauce
¼ teaspoon garlic powder
½ teaspoon oregano
¼ teaspoon basil
12 hamburger buns, split
6 slices provolone cheese

....

To browned turkey, add onion, green chilies,
tomato sauce, garlic powder, oregano, and basil.
Bring to boil over high heat; reduce heat to
medium and simmer uncovered for 10 minutes,
stirring often. Remove from heat and cool.
Spread 1 bun with ⅓ cup turkey filling. Add a slice
of cheese and top with bun. Continue making
sandwiches until turkey filling is gone. Wrap
sandwiches tightly in foil. Place in freezer bags and
freeze up to 2 months. To serve: Place frozen, foil-
wrapped sandwiches on baking sheet. Bake at 350
degrees for 55 minutes or until heated through.

Freeze food in small portions so it cools
faster and thaws faster for the
tastiest result.

Quick
Tip

HAM & SWISS ON RYE

12 slices rye bread
Mustard to taste
1 pound honey-baked ham
6 slices Swiss cheese

....

On each slice of bread, spread a very thin coating of mustard. Add ham and cheese to 6 of the slices and top each with another slice of bread. Wrap sandwiches in foil and place in large freezer bag. Freeze up to 2 weeks. To serve: Remove from freezer in the morning and it will be thawed by lunchtime.

TURKEY & BACON WRAPS

6 (8 inch) corn tortillas
2 tablespoons butter, softened
1 pound deli turkey
6 slices bacon, cooked
6 slices American cheese

Spread tortillas with softened butter and top with turkey, bacon, and cheese. Roll up and cut in half. Wrap individually in foil and freeze several in large freezer bag. Freeze up to 1 month. To serve: Remove from freezer in the morning and it will be thawed by lunchtime.

ITALIAN COLD CUT SANDWICH

½ cup prepared basil pesto
12 slices Italian bread
1 pound deli ham
1 pound deli salami
6 slices provolone cheese

Spread thin layer of pesto on each slice of bread. Add ham, salami, and cheese to 6 of the slices and top each with another slice of bread. Wrap sandwiches in foil and place in large freezer bag. Freeze up to 2 weeks. To serve: Remove from freezer in the morning and it will be thawed by lunchtime.

PEANUT BUTTER & JELLY

2 slices bread
2 to 3 teaspoons peanut butter
1 teaspoon jelly

....

Spread each slice of bread with a thick coating of peanut butter. (You must spread the peanut butter on each slice of bread, or the jelly will soak through and make the thawed sandwich soggy.) Spread jelly on top of peanut butter on only one of the slices. Cover with the other slice and place in sealable sandwich bag. Freeze up to 3 months. Make several of these sandwiches to keep handy for mornings when you're running late.

TURKEY BACON SANDWICH

½ cup prepared basil pesto
12 slices whole-wheat bread
1 pound deli turkey
6 slices bacon, cooked
6 slices Swiss cheese

....

Spread thin layer of pesto on each slice of bread. Add turkey, bacon, and cheese to 6 of the slices and top with another slice of bread. Wrap sandwiches in foil and place in large freezer bag. Freeze up to 2 weeks. To serve: Remove from freezer in the morning and it will be thawed by lunchtime.

PEANUT BUTTER GRANOLA WRAP

1 cup crunchy peanut butter
1 cup granola cereal
2 tablespoons honey
6 (8 inch) whole-wheat tortillas
2 tablespoons butter, softened

In medium bowl, combine peanut butter, granola, and honey. Mix well. Spread tortillas with softened butter then spread with peanut butter mixture. Roll up tortillas and cut in half. Wrap in foil and freeze in large freezer bags. Freeze up to 1 month. To serve: Remove from freezer in the morning and it will be thawed by lunchtime.

CHICKEN PESTO WRAP

LUNCHES

1/4 cup ranch salad dressing
1/3 cup basil pesto
1/4 cup grated Parmesan cheese
1 1/2 cups cooked chicken, chopped
6 (8 inch) corn tortillas
3 tablespoons butter, softened

In medium bowl, combine dressing, pesto, and cheese. Mix well. Add chicken and stir to mix. Spread each tortilla with softened butter and top with chicken mixture. Roll up and cut in half. Wrap in foil and freeze in large freezer bags. Freeze up to 1 month. To serve: Remove from freezer in the morning and it will be thawed by lunchtime.

TEX-MEX ROLL-UPS

1 (15 ounce) can refried beans
1 cup chunky salsa
1 (15 ounce) can kidney beans, rinsed and drained
2 cups cheddar jack cheese
6 (8 inch) corn tortillas

In medium bowl, combine refried beans and salsa. Mix well. Stir in kidney beans and cheese. Spread on tortillas. Roll up and cut in half. Wrap individually in foil and freeze several in large freezer bag. Freeze up to 1 month. To serve: Remove from freezer in the morning and it will be thawed by lunchtime. You can also warm a thawed wrap in the microwave for 30 seconds to melt the cheese.

BAKING DISH CONSERVATION

If you're freezing several casseroles for the coming weeks and months, but don't have many baking dishes to store them in, line a baking dish with heavy-duty foil before assembling the casserole. Fill the dish, freeze, then remove the foil-wrapped food and seal it in a heavy-duty freezer bag and return it to the freezer. To serve, remove the foil package from the freezer bag and place it in the original baking dish to thaw and bake.

Quick Tip

HAM & CHEESE WRAPS

6 (8 inch) corn tortillas
2 tablespoons butter, softened
1 pound deli ham
6 slices cheddar cheese

....

Spread tortillas with softened butter and top
with ham and cheese. Roll up and cut in half.
Wrap individually in foil and freeze several in
large freezer bag. Freeze up to 1 month. To serve:
Remove from freezer in the morning and it will be
thawed by lunchtime.

CHILI MAC

1 (14 ounce) box macaroni and cheese,
   prepared according to package instructions
½ pound ground beef, browned and drained
1 (14 ounce) can diced tomatoes with onions

· ·

In large bowl, mix all ingredients together and
place in freezable storage container. Freeze up to
2 months. To serve: Heat in microwavable dish 5
minutes on medium-high.

TURKEY & MUENSTER SANDWICHES

Mustard
12 slices bread
1 pound deli turkey
6 slices Muenster cheese

....

Spread thin layer of mustard onto each slice of
bread. Add turkey and cheese to 6 slices and top
each with another slice of bread. Wrap individually
in foil and place in large freezer bags. Freeze up
to 2 weeks. To serve: Remove from freezer in the
morning and it will be thawed by lunchtime.

BEEF & BACON SANDWICHES

4 ounces cream cheese, softened
2 tablespoons horseradish
12 slices bread
6 slices bacon, cooked
1 pound deli roast beef

....

In mixing bowl, combine cream cheese and horseradish. Mix well. Spread mixture evenly onto each slice of bread. Add bacon and beef to half the slices and top each with another slice of bread. Wrap individually in foil and place in large freezer bags. Freeze up to 2 weeks. To serve: Remove from freezer in the morning and it will be thawed by lunchtime.

HAM & CHEESE SANDWICHES

Mustard
1 loaf whole-wheat bread
Deli ham
Sliced cheese

....

Spread thin layer of mustard on each slice of bread. Add ham and cheese to half the slices and top each with another slice of bread. Seal in individual sandwich bags and store several sandwiches in larger freezer bag. Freeze up to 1 month. To serve: Remove from freezer in the morning and it will be thawed by lunchtime.

LUNCHES

BOLOGNA SANDWICHES

12 slices white bread
Mustard
1 pound bologna
6 slices cheddar cheese

....

Spread each slice of bread with thin layer of
mustard. Top half the slices with bologna, cheese,
and another slice of bread. Wrap individually in
foil and place in large freezer bags. Freeze up to
2 weeks. To serve: Remove from freezer in the
morning and it will be thawed by lunchtime.

PEANUT BUTTER & BANANA SANDWICHES

2 slices bread
2 to 3 teaspoons peanut butter
½ small banana, sliced thin

....

Spread each slice of bread with thick coating of peanut butter. Top one with sliced banana. Cover with the other slice and place in sealable sandwich bag. Freeze up to 2 weeks. To serve: Remove from freezer in the morning and it will be thawed by lunchtime.

CAFÉ-STYLE SANDWICHES

4 ounces cream cheese, softened
¼ cup black olives, sliced
¼ cup sun-dried tomatoes
12 slices bread
1 pound deli ham

....

In mixing bowl, combine cream cheese, olives, and tomatoes. Mix well. Spread mixture evenly onto each slice of bread. Add ham to half the slices and top each with another slice of bread. Wrap in foil and place in large freezer bags. Freeze up to 2 weeks. To serve: Remove from freezer in the morning and it will be thawed by lunchtime.

BEST IF USED BY...

Use this handy chart as a quick reference for how long these types of food generally hold up in the freezer:

Tomato/vegetable sauces	6 months
Meat loaf (any type of meat)	6 months
Soups and stews	2 to 3 months
Poultry and meat casseroles	6 months
Poultry (cooked, no gravy)	3 months
Poultry (with gravy/sauce)	5 to 6 months
Meatballs in sauce	6 months
Pizza dough (raw, homemade)	3 to 4 weeks
Muffins/quick breads (baked)	2 to 3 months

SANTA FE CHICKEN SANDWICHES

¼ cup prepared basil pesto
12 slices Italian bread
1 pound deli-sliced oven roasted chicken
6 slices bacon, cooked
6 slices cheddar cheese

....

Spread thin layer of pesto on each slice of bread. Add chicken, bacon, and cheese to half the slices and top each with another slice of bread. Wrap individually in foil and place in large freezer bags. Freeze up to 2 weeks. To serve: Remove from freezer in the morning and it will be thawed by lunchtime.

Dinner Meals

He who despises his neighbor sins, but blessed is he who is kind to the needy.

PROVERBS 14:21

BEEF & NOODLE CASSEROLE

8 ounces egg noodles
8 ounces cream cheese
½ cup sour cream
½ cup cheddar cheese, shredded
16 ounces cottage cheese
1 small sweet onion, chopped
2 cups tomato sauce
2 pounds lean ground beef, browned and drained

Cook noodles according to package directions until almost tender. Drain and set aside. In large bowl, mix together cream cheese, sour cream, cheddar cheese, and cottage cheese. Add onion and set aside. Add tomato sauce to ground beef. Grease 9x13-inch freezable baking dish, and arrange casserole in the following layers: noodles, cheese mixture, meat mixture. Repeat. Top with cheese. Double wrap casserole in aluminum foil and freeze up to 2 months. To serve: Allow to thaw overnight. Bake at 375 degrees for 30 minutes.

HONEY MUSTARD PORK CHOPS

½ cup honey
2 tablespoons prepared mustard
6 boneless pork chops, ¼ pound each

· ·

Mix honey and mustard together. Spray 9x13-inch freezable baking dish with cooking spray. Place pork chops in dish and spread with honey-mustard mixture. Cover pan tightly with aluminum foil and freeze up to 2 months. To serve: Thaw overnight in refrigerator. Bake at 425 degrees for 25 minutes or until pork chops are no longer pink inside.

HERBED CHICKEN WITH BACON

4 ounces cream cheese, softened
1 teaspoon garlic powder
1 teaspoon basil
$\frac{1}{8}$ teaspoon pepper
12 fresh boneless, skinless chicken breasts,
   cut into strips
1 pound bacon
1 tablespoon butter

··

In bowl, combine cream cheese, garlic powder, basil, and pepper. Set aside. Arrange chicken strips on baking sheet lined with wax paper. Top each piece with an even amount of cream cheese mixture, then top with another chicken strip. Wrap strips of bacon around each piece of chicken. Flash freeze by allowing each to freeze for 30 minutes. Wrap individually in wax paper and store in large freezer bag. Freeze up to 3 months. To serve: Thaw in refrigerator overnight. In large skillet, melt butter and add chicken. Cook for 3 minutes on medium heat and turn over. Cover and cook on low heat for 8 minutes or until done in center. Serve with vegetables.

PESTO HAMBURGERS

3 eggs
3 pieces dry toast, crumbed
1 large sweet onion, chopped
1 cup Parmesan cheese
6 tablespoons basil pesto
2 teaspoons garlic powder
3 pounds fresh lean ground beef

In large bowl, combine eggs, toast crumbs, onion, cheese, pesto, and garlic powder. Mix well. Add ground beef and mix well. Divide mixture into 12 burgers. Flash freeze on cookie sheet by allowing to freeze for 30 minutes, then transfer burgers to freezer bags. To serve: Allow to thaw overnight in refrigerator. Grill burgers until center is no longer pink. Serve on buns and with french fries.

LASAGNA

1 pound lean ground beef, browned
1 small onion, chopped
2 (28 ounce) jars chunky spaghetti sauce
2 (15 ounce) containers ricotta cheese
2 cups sharp cheddar cheese, shredded
2 eggs
1 tablespoon oregano
2 teaspoons garlic salt
6 cups mozzarella cheese, shredded
2 (16 ounce) packages no-boil lasagna noodles

Brown ground beef with onion, add spaghetti sauce. In seperate bowl combine ricotta cheese, cheddar cheese, eggs, oregano, and garlic salt. Mix well. In bottom of 2 lined lasagna dishes, spoon ¼ cup of the sauce. Layer uncooked noodles, ricotta mixture, mozzarella cheese, and spaghetti sauce mixture into the dishes. Repeat layers until all ingredients are used, ending with sauce topped with a generous sprinkling of mozzarella cheese. Cover with foil and freeze. To serve: Thaw overnight in refrigerator. Bake at 350 degrees for 1 hour.

CHICKEN FETTUCCINE

1 pound ground chicken
1 large sweet onion, chopped
2 (14 ounce) cans diced tomatoes
2 teaspoons oregano
1 teaspoon sugar
1 teaspoon salt
1/4 teaspoon pepper
8 ounces whole-grain fettuccine noodles
2 cups mozzarella cheese

Brown ground chicken with onion in large skillet. Add tomatoes, oregano, sugar, salt, and pepper. Mix well. Allow to cool. Pour into freezer container and freeze up to 3 months. To serve: Thaw overnight in refrigerator. Prepare fettuccine noodles according to package instructions. Place fettuccine in 9x13-inch baking dish, pour chicken mixture over top, and bake at 350 degrees for 45 minutes. Sprinkle with mozzarella cheese and cook 5 additional minutes or until cheese is melted.

PIZZA PASTA

2 pounds ground beef, browned
1 small onion, chopped and drained
2 (28 ounce) jars chunky spaghetti sauce
1 (16 ounce) package rotini pasta, cooked
   according to package instructions to al dente
4 cups shredded mozzarella cheese
8 ounces sliced turkey pepperoni

....

Spray two 9x13-inch freezable baking dishes with cooking spray. Divide beef, sauce, and pasta evenly into both dishes. Mix well. Sprinkle with cheese and top with pepperoni. Cover tightly with foil and freeze up to 3 months. To serve: Thaw casserole in refrigerator overnight. Bake at 350 degrees for 35 minutes or until heated through.

SHARING WITH OTHERS

There's no more thoughtful way to share your blessings with others than by making a couple of extra freezer meals each month to take to someone in need!

Quick Tip

SPINACH MANICOTTI

$\frac{1}{2}$ cup mozzarella cheese, shredded
16 ounces ricotta cheese
1 egg white, beaten
1 (10 ounce) package frozen chopped spinach,
    cooked according to package instructions
    and drained
Salt and pepper to taste
1 (8 ounce) package manicotti shells,
    cooked according to package instructions
2 to 3 cups marinara sauce

Combine mozzarella cheese, ricotta cheese, egg white, spinach, salt, and pepper. Stuff mixture into shells. Place in 9x13-inch baking dish. Cover with foil and freeze up to 3 months. To serve: Thaw overnight in refrigerator. Top with marinara sauce and bake at 350 degrees for 40 minutes or until done.

TEX-MEX CHICKEN CASSEROLE

1 (9 ounce) package frozen, fully cooked,
  diced chicken breast
1 onion, chopped
1 teaspoon garlic salt
1 tablespoon olive oil
2 (15 ounce) cans black beans, drained and rinsed
1 (24 ounce) jar chunky salsa
1 cup taco sauce
8 corn tortillas
1 cup sour cream
2 cups cheddar jack cheese, shredded

In large bowl, combine frozen chicken, onion, garlic salt, olive oil, black beans, and salsa. Pour taco sauce into freezable baking dish. Layer four corn tortillas over sauce. Top with half of chicken mixture. Spoon on half of sour cream. Sprinkle with half of cheese. Repeat layers once. Cover with foil and freeze up to 3 months. To serve: Thaw casserole overnight in refrigerator. Bake covered at 350 degrees for 40 minutes until bubbly. Uncover and bake 10 additional minutes until cheese melts.

TURKEY ENCHILADAS

1 pound ground turkey
1 small onion, chopped
1 cup sour cream
1 cup frozen whole kernel corn
2 cups enchilada sauce, divided
2 cups shredded cheddar jack cheese, divided
6 (8 inch) wheat tortillas

Brown turkey with onion. In large bowl, combine turkey mixture, sour cream, corn, and ¼ cup enchilada sauce. Spread ⅓ cup enchilada sauce in greased 9x13-inch baking dish. Spoon 2 tablespoons meat mixture and 1 tablespoon cheese on each tortilla and roll up. Place seam side down in baking dish. Pour remaining enchilada sauce evenly over tortillas. Sprinkle with remaining cheese. Double wrap dish in foil and freeze up to 3 months. To serve: Thaw overnight in refrigerator. Bake at 350 degrees for 30 minutes. Remove foil and bake an additional 5 minutes or until cheese is melted.

STUFFED PEPPERS

4 green peppers
1 pound lean ground beef
2 cups white rice, cooked
1 small onion, chopped
1 ½ teaspoons salt
⅛ teaspoon pepper
1 (16 ounce) jar tomato sauce, divided
2 cups cheddar jack cheese, shredded

....

Cut tops off peppers and discard. Remove seeds and wash. Combine beef, rice, onion, salt, pepper, and ½ cup sauce. Stuff peppers with rice mixture and set in large baking dish. Pour remaining sauce over peppers. Top with cheese. Allow to cool. Double wrap in foil and freeze up to 1 month. To serve: Allow to sit at room temperature, covered, for 30 minutes. Then bake at 425 degrees for 1 hour. Uncover peppers and bake an additional 20 minutes or until done.

MACARONI & CHEESE

8 ounces macaroni noodles, cooked al dente
   according to package instructions
6 tablespoons butter, divided
6 tablespoons flour
3 cups milk
Salt and pepper to taste
1½ cups cheddar cheese
2 cups fresh bread crumbs

To hot noodles, add 1 tablespoon butter. Cover
and set aside. In small saucepan, melt remaining
butter, add flour, and stir over medium heat about
30 seconds. Do not allow to brown. Add milk
and whisk until mixture thickens. Season with salt
and pepper. Reduce heat and simmer. Add cheese,
stirring until melted. Toss mixture with macaroni
noodles and place in freezable casserole dish.
Top with bread crumbs. Allow to cool. Cover and
freeze up to 3 months. To serve: Allow to thaw
at room temperature for 1 hour. Bake at 350
degrees for 45 minutes.

TURKEY & STUFFING CASSEROLE

3 (8 ounce) packages stuffing mix
3 cups water
3 tablespoons melted butter
10 cups cubed cooked turkey
3 cups cheddar cheese, shredded
1 (14 ounce) can cream of celery soup
1 (8 ounce) can mushrooms, drained
1 (12 ounce) can evaporated milk

In large bowl, combine all ingredients and mix well. Divide evenly into 3 greased 9x13-inch freezable pans. Cover and freeze up to 3 months. To serve: Thaw overnight in the refrigerator. Bake uncovered at 350 degrees for 35 minutes or until bubbly. Add chicken broth if casserole seems dry. Let stand 10 minutes before serving.

CHICKEN & BROCCOLI BAKE

1 (10 ounce) package frozen broccoli florets
1 cup sharp cheddar cheese, shredded
2 cups chicken, cooked and cubed
Salt and pepper to taste
1 cup cooked rice
1 teaspoon garlic salt
1 (14 ounce) can cream of chicken soup
1 cup sour cream

....

In large bowl, combine all ingredients and mix well.
Pour into 9x13-inch freezable baking dish. Cover
with heavy-duty foil and freeze up to 3 months. To
serve: Thaw overnight in refrigerator and bake at
400 degrees for 30 minutes or until bubbly.

HEALTHY PASTA CASSEROLE

2 pounds lean ground beef
1 large onion, chopped
4 cloves garlic, minced
2 cups water
1 large tomato, chopped
1 large carrot, chopped
2 (28 ounce) jars spaghetti sauce
1 (16 ounce) package rotini pasta,
    cooked and drained
4 cups low-fat mozzarella cheese, shredded

In large skillet, cook beef, onion, and garlic until meat is no longer pink. Drain. Add water, tomato, and carrot. Allow to boil. Stir in spaghetti sauce and pasta. Transfer to 2 greased 9x13-inch freezable baking dishes. Sprinkle with cheese. Cover and freeze up to 3 months. To serve: Thaw in refrigerator overnight. Bake at 350 degrees for 35 to 40 minutes or until heated through.

FREEZER TEMPERATURE

Your freezer temperature should be below 0 degrees Fahrenheit. The faster food freezes the smaller the ice crystals. The smaller the ice crystals, the smaller the change in texture, which means better quality when thawed.

TURKEY &
WILD RICE BAKE

3 cups wild rice, undercooked by 10 minutes
3 cups turkey (or chicken), chopped and cooked
1 (16 ounce) package frozen french-cut
  green beans
1 (17 ounce) jar 4-cheese Alfredo sauce
½ cup butter cracker crumbs

Mix all ingredients except cracker crumbs and place in freezable baking dish. Cover tightly with foil and freeze up to 3 months. To serve: Thaw casserole overnight in refrigerator. Uncover, sprinkle with butter cracker crumbs. Bake at 350 degrees for 50 to 65 minutes until heated through.

CHILI BAKE

2 cups white rice, cooked
1 cup milk
2 eggs, beaten
1 (4 ounce) can diced green chilies
1 (15 ounce) can pinto beans, drained
2 cups Monterey Jack cheese, shredded

In large bowl, mix all ingredients and pour into greased freezable casserole dish. Cover tightly with foil and freeze up to 3 months. To serve: Thaw casserole overnight in refrigerator. Stir well and top with additional cheese if desired. Bake at 350 degrees for 60 minutes until set.

CHICKEN BAKE

1 (10 ounce) can cream of chicken soup
1 cup sour cream
¼ cup milk
2 cups chicken, cooked and cubed
3 cups sharp cheddar cheese, shredded and
   divided
3½ cups frozen hash brown potatoes
1½ cups frozen peppers and onions

Combine soup, sour cream, milk, chicken, and
half of the cheese. Spread ¾ of this mixture in
a greased freezable baking dish. Sprinkle hash
browns and peppers and onions over top of
casserole and press down lightly with fork. Top
vegetables with remaining soup mixture. Sprinkle
with remaining cheese. Wrap in heavy-duty
foil and freeze up to 3 months. To serve: Thaw
overnight in refrigerator. Uncover and bake at 350
degrees for 60 minutes until bubbly and heated
through.

SPAGHETTI BAKE

1 pound lean ground beef
1 small onion, chopped
1 teaspoon garlic salt
1 (12 ounce) package spaghetti, broken into thirds
   and cooked according to package
1 (28 ounce) jar spaghetti sauce
16 ounces ricotta cheese
1 teaspoon oregano
1 cup sharp cheddar cheese, shredded
¼ cup Parmesan cheese

....

Brown ground beef, onion, and garlic salt in skillet.
Drain. Add spaghetti and spaghetti sauce and
simmer, uncovered, for 10 minutes. Allow to cool.
Combine ricotta cheese and oregano. Add to
spaghetti mixture. Pour into 9x13-inch freezable
baking dish. Cover tightly with foil and freeze
up to 3 months. To serve: Thaw overnight in
refrigerator. Cover with cheese. Bake at 325
degrees for 30 minutes or until cooked through.

SPINACH & HERB BURGERS

2 cups sage-seasoned stuffing mix
¾ cup chicken broth
1 pound ground turkey
1 pound lean ground beef
1 (10 ounce) package frozen chopped spinach,
   thawed and squeezed
1 teaspoon salt
½ teaspoon pepper

....

In large bowl, toss stuffing mix with chicken broth
until combined. Add remaining ingredients and mix
well. Shape into patties and place on wax paper
lined cookie sheet. Flash freeze uncovered patties
by allowing them to freeze for about 1 hour. Wrap
in foil and freeze up to 2 months. To serve: Thaw
overnight in refrigerator. Grill or broil until no
longer pink in the center.

NOODLE STROGANOFF

2 tablespoons butter
1 cup mushrooms, sliced
1 small onion, chopped
1 teaspoon garlic salt
1 pound lean ground beef, browned
1 (14 ounce) can beef broth
3 tablespoons lemon juice
3 tablespoons red wine vinegar
1 cup sour cream
1 package egg noodles

In large saucepan, melt butter; sauté mushrooms, onion, and garlic salt. Add ground beef, beef broth, lemon juice, and red wine vinegar, and pour into 9x13-inch pan. Cover and freeze up to 3 months. To serve: Thaw overnight in refrigerator. Bake at 350 degrees for 30 minutes. Stir in 1 cup sour cream and serve with hot buttered noodles.

JUMBO STUFFED SHELLS

1 (10 ounce) can vegetable broth
1 carrot, minced
1 cup fresh broccoli, chopped
1 small onion, chopped fine
2 cups ricotta cheese
1 cup mozzarella cheese, shredded
1 egg
½ cup Parmesan cheese, grated
1 teaspoon oregano
¼ teaspoon basil
24 jumbo pasta shells, cooked according to
    package instructions
Spaghetti sauce

In large saucepan, heat broth to boiling. Stir in vegetables and cook 4 minutes or until almost tender. Drain. Combine vegetable mixture with ricotta, mozzarella, egg, Parmesan cheese, and herbs. Fill each cooled pasta shell with cheese mixture. Cool completely and place individual shells in sealable sandwich bags. Place several of these in gallon-size freezer bag and freeze up to 3 months. To serve: Reheat individual shells in microwave on low power 3 minutes. Then top with spaghetti sauce and microwave on medium-high power for 1 to 3 minutes or until hot.

CHILI

1 pound lean ground beef
1 large onion, chopped
1 tablespoon garlic salt
1 tablespoon brown sugar
2 (14 ounce) cans diced tomatoes
1 (15 ounce) can tomato sauce
1 tablespoon chili powder
1 teaspoon ground cumin
1/4 teaspoon red pepper
1 (15 ounce) can pinto beans
1 (15 ounce) can red kidney beans,
   rinsed and drained

....

In large saucepan, brown beef with onion; add remaining ingredients. Bring to boil. Reduce heat, cover and simmer 15 minutes. Cool completely in refrigerator. Place in plastic freezer containers and freeze up to 3 months. To serve: Allow to thaw at room temperature 30 minutes. Place chili in saucepan with 1/4 cup water and cook over medium heat, stirring occasionally, until reheated.

TASTY CASSEROLE TIP

Slightly undercook casseroles that are going to be frozen. They will finish cooking when you are ready to serve.

Quick Tip

DINNER MEALS

KING RANCH CHICKEN CASSEROLE

¼ cup butter or margarine
1 small onion, diced
½ pound mushrooms
1 (14 ounce) can cream of mushroom soup
1 (14 ounce) can cream of chicken soup
1 (15 ounce) can tomatoes
1 (4 ounce) can diced green chilies
1 teaspoon garlic powder
2 tablespoons chili powder
1 tablespoon chicken broth
12 corn tortillas, torn in fourths
2 cups chicken, cooked and diced
4 cups sharp cheddar cheese, shredded

In butter, sauté onion and mushrooms. Add soups, tomatoes, chilies, garlic powder, chili powder, and chicken broth. Line bottom of 9x13-inch baking dish with half the tortilla pieces. Spread half the chicken over the tortillas and top with half the sauce, then half the cheese. Cover with another layer of tortillas and repeat the layers. Cover tightly with foil and freeze up to 2 months. To serve: Thaw overnight in refrigerator. Bake at 350 degrees for 30 minutes.

Sides & Desserts

Humility and the fear of the Lord bring wealth and honor and life.

PROVERBS 22:4

PORK & BEANS

½ pound sliced bacon
2 large sweet onions, chopped
2 garlic cloves, minced
4 (16 ounce) cans pork and beans
½ pound ham, cooked and chunked
1½ cups brown sugar
1 teaspoon parsley
2 medium lemons, juiced
½ cup barbecue sauce
1 teaspoon salt
⅛ teaspoon pepper

Cook bacon in large skillet; remove and set aside.
Cook onions and garlic in drippings until soft.
Remove from heat. Add pork and beans, ham,
brown sugar, parsley, lemon juice, barbecue sauce,
salt, pepper, and reserved cooked bacon. Mix
well and pour into greased freezable baking dish.
Cover and freeze up to 3 months. To serve: Thaw
overnight in refrigerator. Bake at 350 degrees for
40 minutes or until bubbly.

ITALIAN PASTA SALAD

1 cup water
1 large carrot, peeled and chopped
1 cup fresh broccoli, chopped
1½ cups dry rotini, undercooked by 3 minutes
½ cup zesty Italian salad dressing
1 cup Parmesan cheese

Bring water to boil in saucepan. Add carrot and broccoli. Boil 3 to 5 minutes until carrot pieces begin to get tender. Drain and combine with remaining ingredients. Mix well. Freeze in individual-portion servings in freezer containers. To serve: Remove from freezer in the morning and it will be thawed by lunchtime.

FREEZER COLESLAW

1 medium head cabbage, shredded
1 teaspoon salt
3 large carrots, grated
1 small sweet onion, sliced thin
2 cups sugar
¼ cup water
1 cup apple cider vinegar
1 teaspoon celery seed
½ teaspoon mustard seed

Combine cabbage, salt, carrots, and onion. Toss and refrigerate for 1 hour. Meanwhile, bring sugar, water, and vinegar to boil. Remove from heat and stir in celery seed and mustard seed. Cool completely. Pour over cabbage mixture and cover. Freeze up to 2 months. To serve: Thaw slightly in refrigerator. Serve cold.

GARLIC RANCH MASHED POTATOES

2 pounds potatoes, peeled and diced
¾ cup milk
6 tablespoons butter
1 tablespoon garlic salt
2 tablespoons ranch dressing

Boil potatoes until soft. Mash with remaining ingredients. Scoop into muffin pans and flash freeze by allowing to freeze for 30 minutes. Once frozen, remove from muffin pans and freeze in individual sandwich bags placed in gallon-size freezer bags. To serve: Defrost and heat as many servings as you need in the microwave.

CREAMED CORN

18 cups corn, cut off the cob
1 pound butter
1 pint half-and-half
1 tablespoon freezer salt
1 tablespoon sugar

....

Mix all ingredients together in large roasting pan.
Bake uncovered 1 hour at 325 degrees. Stir every
15 minutes. It's normal for this to look slightly
curdled. Allow to cool. Package in freezer bags or
containers. Freeze up to 6 months. To serve: Thaw
in refrigerator or microwave. Heat until warm.

FREEZER PICKLES

7 cups small cucumbers, sliced thin
3 medium sweet onions, sliced
2 cups sugar
1 cup vinegar
½ teaspoon celery seed
1 tablespoon salt

Mix all ingredients in large bowl. Refrigerate
24 hours. Put in containers and freeze up to 3
months. To serve: Defrost and serve cold.

BROCCOLI RICE CASSEROLE

1 large onion, chopped and sautéed in butter with
1 teaspoon garlic salt 1 (10 ounce) package frozen
   chopped broccoli
2 tablespoons butter
1 (15 ounce) can cream of mushroom soup
2 cups cheddar cheese, shredded
3 cups cooked white rice

In saucepan, heat butter, sauté onion and garlic salt. In large bowl, mix remaining ingredients together well; add sauté mixture. Pour into freezable baking dish and cover tightly. Freeze up to 3 months. To serve: Thaw overnight in refrigerator and bake at 350 degrees for 30 minutes.

BAKING PRODUCTS THAT LAST

Baking products can be expensive, and you don't want anything to go to waste. If you don't bake very often or like to buy your baking ingredients in bulk, you can keep many products like baking chocolate, baking chips, flour, nuts, dried fruits, butter, marshmallows, and cream cheese in the freezer until you are ready to use them.

Quick
Tip

STUFFED BAKED POTATOES

8 baking potatoes, baked
2 tablespoons butter
¾ cup milk
I egg, slightly beaten
I cup cheddar cheese, shredded
3 tablespoons fresh chives, chopped
Salt and pepper to taste

Cut baked potatoes in half lengthwise. Scoop out center of each potato and put in large mixing bowl. Add butter, milk, and egg and beat with electric mixer until smooth. Add cheese, chives, salt, and pepper, and mix well. Heap back into potato skins. Place filled potatoes on cookie sheet and flash freeze by allowing them to freeze for 30 minutes. Put in individual sandwich bags inside gallon-size freezer bags. To serve: Thaw completely and bake at 350 degrees for 25 minutes.

ORANGE DREAM PIE

⅔ cup orange juice
1 (3 ounce) package orange-flavored gelatin
1 cup vanilla ice cream, softened
1 (11 ounce) can Mandarin oranges, drained
1 cup whipped topping
1 deep-dish refrigerated piecrust, baked

··

Bring orange juice to boil and dissolve gelatin. Add
ice cream gradually, blending until dissolved. Chill 1
hour. Stir in Mandarin oranges and fold in whipped
topping. Pour into piecrust. Freeze up to 2
months. Remove from freezer 15 minutes before
serving.

PINK CRANBERRY SALAD

8 ounces cream cheese, softened
2 tablespoons mayonnaise
2 tablespoons sugar
1 (16 ounce) can whole cranberry sauce
1 (9 ounce) can crushed pineapple, drained
2 cups whipped topping

Combine cream cheese, mayonnaise, and sugar. Add cranberry sauce and pineapple. Stir. Fold in whipped topping. Pour into oblong or square freezable container. Cover and freeze up to 2 months. To serve: Allow to sit at room temperature 30 minutes. Cut into squares.

CHOCOLATE RASPBERRY CREAM PIE

8 ounces cream cheese, softened
1 (7 ounce) jar marshmallow crème
1 cup raspberry sherbet, softened
2 cups whipped topping
1 (9 inch) prepared chocolate piecrust

Beat cream cheese and marshmallow crème until well blended. Fold in sherbet and whipped topping. Spoon into piecrust. Cover and freeze up to 2 months. Remove from freezer about 10 to 15 minutes before serving.

SIDES & DESSERTS

CREAMY CHOCOLATE PIE

SIDES & DESSERTS

¾ cup semisweet chocolate chips
3 ounces cream cheese, softened
⅓ cup sugar
2 tablespoons milk
⅛ teaspoon salt
I cup whipped topping
I (9 inch) prepared chocolate piecrust

Melt chocolate chips in microwave in 30-second intervals until melted. Blend chocolate, cream cheese, sugar, milk, and salt until smooth. Fold in whipped topping. Pour into piecrust. Cover and freeze up to 2 months. Remove from freezer about 10 to 15 minutes before serving.

CHOCOLATE MOUSSE PIE

2 (16 ounce) bags semisweet chocolate chips
2 (8 ounce) packages cream cheese, softened
8 cups whipped topping
2 (14 ounce) cans sweetened condensed milk
4 (9 inch) prepared chocolate piecrusts

In large bowl, melt chocolate chips in microwave in 30-second intervals until melted. Add cream cheese, whipped topping, and milk to chocolate. Mix on low speed until smooth. Pour into piecrusts and freeze up to 1 month. Remove from freezer 10 to 15 minutes before serving.

CHOCOLATE CHIP PEANUT BUTTER PIE

1 quart vanilla ice cream
1 cup peanut butter, melted
1 teaspoon vanilla
½ pint whipping cream, beaten until stiff
1 cup mini chocolate chips
2 (8 inch) graham cracker piecrusts

Spoon ice cream into large bowl. Allow to soften slightly. Stir in peanut butter and vanilla until mixed. Fold in whipped cream and mini chocolate chips. Pour into piecrusts and cover. Freeze up to 2 months. Remove from freezer about 10 to 15 minutes before serving.

KISS COOKIES

¼ cup butter, softened (no substitutions)
¼ cup shortening
½ cup brown sugar, packed
½ cup granulated sugar
½ teaspoon vanilla
1 egg
½ cup peanut butter
1⅓ cups flour
1 teaspoon baking soda
¼ teaspoon salt
60 milk chocolate kisses

Cream together butter, shortening, sugars, and vanilla. Beat in egg. Add peanut butter and mix well. Mix in flour, baking soda, and salt. Shape dough into two 8-inch logs on wax paper. Cover with wax paper and then again in heavy-duty foil. Freeze up to 3 months. To serve: Unwrap logs and allow to sit at room temperature 15 minutes. Slice frozen logs into ¼-inch slices. Bake on cookie sheets at 350 degrees for 8 minutes. Gently press one chocolate kiss in center of each cookie. Bake an additional 2 minutes or until lightly browned. Remove to wire rack to cool.

SIDES & DESSERTS

COOL DOWN

Allow hot foods to cool before freezing.
When you first place cooled food in the
freezer, leave plenty of space around the
container so cold air can circulate around
it. This allows it to freeze faster and
taste better when it's reheated. Once it's
completely frozen, it can be stacked with
the rest of the items in the freezer.

Quick
Tip

CHOCOLATE COOKIE DELIGHT

28 chocolate sandwich cookies, crushed
½ cup butter, melted
½ gallon vanilla ice cream
1 (12 ounce) can evaporated milk
1 teaspoon vanilla
1 (6 ounce) package chocolate chips
6 tablespoons butter
4 cups whipped topping

Combine crushed cookies with butter and press into 9x13-inch freezable dish. Flash freeze by allowing to freeze 30 minutes. Soften ice cream and spread over frozen cookie layer. Freeze an additional hour. Bring evaporated milk, vanilla, chocolate chips, and butter to boil for 1 minute. Cool and fold in whipped topping. Spread over ice cream and freeze up to 2 months. Serve frozen.

SIDES & DESSERTS

FROSTY PUMPKIN DESSERT

20 gingersnap cookies, crushed and divided
1 (16 ounce) can pumpkin
½ cup sugar
½ teaspoon salt
½ teaspoon cinnamon
¼ teaspoon nutmeg
1 quart vanilla ice cream, softened

Line 8x8-inch freezable dish with half of cookie crumbs. Mix pumpkin, sugar, salt, cinnamon, and nutmeg. Blend pumpkin mixture with softened ice cream on low speed. Spread half the pumpkin mixture into crumb-lined dish. Sprinkle half of remaining crumbs over this layer. Add another layer of pumpkin mixture and top with remaining crumbs. Freeze up to 2 months.
Serve frozen.

LEMON SUGAR COOKIES

3 cups flour
2 teaspoons baking powder
½ teaspoon salt
2 cups sugar
1 cup shortening
2 eggs
¼ cup lemon juice
Additional sugar for rolling

In small bowl, stir together flour, baking powder, and salt; set aside. In large mixing bowl, beat sugar and shortening until fluffy; beat in eggs. Stir in dry ingredients. Add lemon juice and mix well. Shape into two 8-inch logs on wax paper. Wrap in wax paper and then place in freezer bag. Freeze up to 3 months. To serve: Slice frozen cookies, roll in sugar, and bake at 375 degrees for 12 minutes.

CHOCOLATE CHIP COOKIE DOUGH

1 cup butter-flavored shortening
10 tablespoons granulated sugar
10 tablespoons light brown sugar
1 teaspoon vanilla
2 eggs
2 cups plus 2 tablespoons flour
1 teaspoon baking soda
1 (16 ounce) package chocolate chips

Cream together shortening, sugars, vanilla, and eggs. Combine flour and soda and stir into creamed mixture. Blend well. Stir in chocolate chips. Shape into two 8-inch logs on wax paper. Wrap in wax paper and then place in freezer bag. Freeze up to 3 months. To serve: Slice frozen cookies and bake at 375 degrees for 12 minutes.

FUDGE

3 cups semisweet chocolate chips
1 (14 ounce) can sweetened condensed milk
1 teaspoon vanilla

....

In large microwavable bowl, combine chocolate chips and sweetened condensed milk. Microwave on high 2 minutes. Add vanilla. Stir. Line an 8x8-inch pan with wax paper and pour in fudge. Flash freeze by allowing to freeze 30 minutes. Remove from pan and wrap in wax paper. Store in large freezer bag and freeze up to 3 months.

OLD-FASHIONED WALNUT BALLS

1 cup butter
⅓ cup brown sugar
1 teaspoon vanilla
2 cups flour
½ teaspoon salt
1½ cups walnuts, chopped fine
Powdered sugar

....

In large bowl, cream butter, sugar, and vanilla until fluffy. Sift flour and salt together; add to creamed mixture. Mix well; stir in walnuts. Shape dough into walnut-size balls. Bake at 375 degrees on ungreased cookie sheet 12 to 15 minutes. Remove from cookie sheet. While still warm but cool enough to handle, roll in powdered sugar. Freeze up to 6 months.

JEANNE'S OATMEAL COOKIE DOUGH

1 cup brown sugar, firmly packed
¾ cup shortening
½ cup granulated sugar
1 egg
¼ cup water
1 teaspoon vanilla
3 cups quick oats, uncooked
1 cup flour
1 teaspoon salt
½ teaspoon baking soda

....

In large bowl, beat brown sugar, shortening, and sugar until creamy. Add egg, water, and vanilla; beat well. Add oats, flour, salt, and baking soda; mix well. Shape into two 8-inch logs on wax paper. Wrap in wax paper and then place in freezer bag. Freeze up to 3 months. To serve: Slice frozen cookies and bake at 375 degrees for 12 minutes.

SUGAR COOKIE DOUGH

½ cup butter
1 cup sugar
½ teaspoon vanilla
2 eggs
2 cups flour
2 teaspoons baking powder
¼ teaspoon salt
1 tablespoon milk

In large bowl, cream butter with sugar; add vanilla and eggs. Mix thoroughly. Sift flour and baking powder with salt and add to egg mixture. Add milk and mix well. Shape into two 8-inch logs on wax paper. Wrap in wax paper and then place in freezer bag. Freeze up to 3 months. To serve: Slice frozen cookies and bake at 375 degrees for 12 minutes.

AIR IT OUT

Using a straw, suck out as much air as possible from a freezer bag before freezing.

.... Quick Tip ....

RICH BROWNIE BARS

4 (1 ounce) squares baking chocolate
1 cup butter
2 cups sugar
1 cup flour
4 eggs, beaten
2 teaspoons hot coffee
1 cup semisweet chocolate chips
1 cup chopped nuts

....

Preheat oven to 325 degrees. Grease 9x13-inch baking pan. In small saucepan over low heat, melt chocolate and butter, stirring constantly. Remove from heat. In large bowl, combine sugar and flour. Add chocolate mixture, eggs, and coffee; stir until well blended. Stir in chocolate chips and nuts. Spread batter into prepared pan. Bake 35 minutes; cool. Freeze up to 2 months. Remove from freezer 30 minutes before serving.

More Freezables

By wisdom a house is built, and through understanding it is established; through knowledge its rooms are filled with rare and beautiful treasures.

Proverbs 24:3–4

BABY FOOD

Organic fruits
Organic vegetables

. . . .

Wash produce well and steam each fruit or
vegetable in microwave until soft. Blend in food
processor until completely pureed. Spoon into
clean, dry ice cube trays. Each cube is 1 serving
size. Flash freeze by allowing trays to freeze for
30 minutes; then remove food cubes from trays
to place in individual, labeled, freezer bags. Freeze
up to 3 months. To serve: Remove desired amount
and warm slightly in microwave. Make sure the
food is not too hot for baby!

MORE FREEZABLES

CHUNKY PIZZA SAUCE

1 (28 ounce) can crushed tomatoes
1 small onion, chopped fine
1 large carrot, chopped fine
1 (6 ounce) can tomato paste
2 tablespoons sugar
1 teaspoon basil
1 teaspoon oregano
1 teaspoon garlic powder
1 teaspoon onion powder
Dash pepper

In large saucepan, combine all ingredients and bring to boil, stirring frequently. Reduce heat and simmer 45 minutes. Allow to cool. Freeze in freezer containers up to 6 months.

SALSA

12 large tomatoes, cored
¼ cup olive oil
8 ounces diced green chilies
2 tablespoons garlic salt
2 large sweet onions, chopped fine
3 tablespoons fresh lime juice
¼ teaspoon salt

....

Blanch tomatoes by dropping in boiling water 1 minute. Place blanched tomatoes in ice-cold water for 3 minutes. Peel skins and remove excess juice. Chop tomatoes and place in colander, pressing them firmly to force out remaining juice. Blot tomatoes on paper towel and place in large saucepan. Add oil, green chilies, garlic salt, onions, lime juice, salt, and pepper. Cover and simmer 10 minutes, stirring every minute or two. Cool and place into freezer containers. Freeze up to 6 months. To serve: Thaw and serve with tortilla chips.

4 cups fresh strawberries
1 (3 ounce) box sugar-free pectin
1 cup sugar
1 cup unsweetened white grape juice

....

Wash strawberries and remove stems. Chop in food processor until berries reach desired consistency. Follow directions for cooked jam on pectin box. Place in freezer jars, and freeze up to 1 year. To serve: Thaw in refrigerator.

MORE FREEZABLES

PARTY MEATBALLS

2 pounds lean ground beef
1 small sweet onion, grated
2 teaspoons garlic salt
⅛ teaspoon pepper
½ cup cornflakes, crushed
2 eggs, beaten
1½ cups chili sauce
Juice of 1 lemon
½ cup grape jelly

In large bowl, thoroughly mix ground beef, onion, garlic salt, pepper, cornflakes, and eggs. Shape into 2-inch balls and place in lightly greased baking dish. In saucepan, combine remaining ingredients and simmer 5 minutes. Pour over meatballs. Bake at 350 degrees for 30 minutes. Allow to cool. Skim off fat and store meatballs in freezer containers. Freeze up to 3 months. To serve: Reheat in slow cooker or microwave.

PIE DOUGH

4 cups flour
1¾ cups shortening
1 tablespoon sugar
2 teaspoons salt
½ cup ice water
1 teaspoon lemon juice
1 egg

Cut in flour and shortening until mixture resembles small peas. Add sugar and salt. Mix well. In separate bowl, beat together ice water, lemon juice, and egg. Add to flour mixture. Mix until ingredients are moist. Divide dough into 5 balls. Wrap each in wax paper and put in freezer bags. To serve: Allow to thaw at room temperature at least 30 minutes before rolling.

BUTTERMILK BISCUITS

4 cups self-rising flour
1 tablespoon sugar
½ cup plus 1 tablespoon butter-flavor shortening
1 package yeast, dissolved in ¾ cup warm water
¾ cup buttermilk

In large bowl, mix flour, sugar, and shortening; add dissolved yeast and buttermilk. Roll out dough on lightly floured surface and cut with biscuit cutter. Bake at 425 degrees for 6 to 8 minutes or until golden. Put in sandwich bags and freeze in gallon-size freezer bags up to 3 months. To serve: Allow to thaw at room temperature 10 minutes. Warm in 300-degree oven for 5 minutes.

Freeze broths, sauces, and other liquids
flat in freezer bags, then stand them up
sideways for storage. They take up less
space in the freezer and will thaw
much faster.

· · · · · · · · · (Quick Tip) · · · · · · · ·

2 quarts fresh strawberries or raspberries
3 cups sugar
1 quart cold water

Wash and stem berries. Dissolve sugar in cold water to make syrup. Place berries in freezer containers and pour syrup over them to about ½ inch from the top of the container. Freeze up to 6 months.

MORE FREEZABLES

Fresh fish, cut into individual servings

Wrap fish tightly in heavy-duty freezer wrap and then store it in freezer bags. Fish can be frozen for up to 3 months. Package with frozen french fries and Freezer Coleslaw and you have a complete meal.

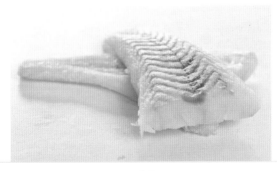

PIZZA CRUST

6½ cups flour, divided
2 packages dry yeast
2 teaspoons salt
2 cups warm water
2 tablespoons cooking oil
1 teaspoon oregano

In mixing bowl, stir together 3 cups of flour, yeast, and salt. Add water and oil. Beat on low for 1 minute. Scrape bowl constantly. Beat 3 minutes on high. Stir in enough of the remaining flour by hand to make a stiff dough. Knead 12 minutes on lightly floured surface until smooth and elastic. Place firm dough in lightly greased bowl. Turn dough over and cover. Let rise 2 hours or until more than doubled in size. Punch down and divide into fourths. Cover and let sit 10 minutes on lightly floured surface. Sprinkle with oregano. Roll each portion to 12-inch circle. Place each on greased 12-inch pizza pan. Bake at 425 degrees for 10 minutes until golden. Remove and let cool on pans. Wrap each crust in foil and freeze. To serve: Top frozen crust with your favorite pizza sauce and other toppings. Bake at 425 degrees for 25 minutes.

CARROTS

1 quart water
½ cup sugar
3 teaspoons canning salt
4 quarts carrots, peeled and chunked

Bring water, sugar, and salt to a boil. Add carrots and simmer 10 minutes. Allow to cool. Place in freezer containers and freeze up to 6 months.

1 cup water
½ cup fresh herb of choice

In blender, combine the water and fresh herbs. Puree until smooth. Pour into ice cube trays and freeze until solid. Remove from trays and place in individual, labeled freezer bags. Keep on hand to flavor soups, stews, salsas, and sauces.

BANANAS

Overripe bananas
Dash lemon juice

. . . .

Mash overripe bananas and add dash of lemon juice. Freeze in freezer bags for up to 6 months. Great for breads, cakes, and muffins.

STRAWBERRY CREAM CHEESE SNACKS

8 ounces cream cheese, softened
$\frac{1}{2}$ cup strawberry jam
12 slices whole-wheat bread

Spread each slice of bread with thick layer of cream cheese. Spread layer of strawberry jam in the center of 6 of the slices. (Make sure jam is not directly touching bread to prevent bread sogginess when thawing.) Top with another slice of bread. Wrap sandwiches in foil and place in large freezer bag. Freeze for up to 1 month. To serve: Remove from freezer and allow 4 hours to thaw.

COFFEE CAKE

Topping:
⅓ cup biscuit baking mix
⅓ cup brown sugar
1 teaspoon cinnamon
2 tablespoons butter, softened

Batter:
2 cups biscuit baking mix
⅓ cup milk
1 egg

Topping: Mix the first three ingredients together. Cut in butter with a fork until mixture is crumbly.

Batter: Mix all the batter ingredients together and spread into greased 8x8-inch pan. Sprinkle with topping. Bake at 375 degrees for 20 minutes or until golden. Eat some warm and freeze the rest for later by wrapping cake in foil and storing in large freezer bag.

Store potato chips in the freezer for a long-lasting crispy snack. Store unpopped popcorn kernels in the freezer and you'll have lighter popcorn with fewer unpopped pieces.

Quick
Tip

Pasta
Sauce

. . . .

Cooked pastas generally lose quality and taste
when frozen. To prevent this from happening,
always undercook the pasta and freeze it in a
sauce for best results. Thaw overnight in the
refrigerator before reheating.

Butter

....

Butter can be frozen for up to 8 months. Freeze it in its original packaging, placed in a heavy-duty freezer bag. When ready to use, just thaw the butter in the refrigerator or microwave. This is a great way to stock up on butter when it's on sale.

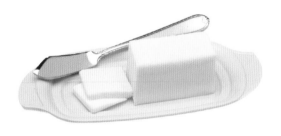

Fresh zucchini
1 tablespoon butter

. . . .

Wash zucchini. Slice into 1-inch pieces. Sauté gently in butter until barely tender. Cool. Pack into plastic containers, leaving 1-inch headspace at the top. Freeze up to 3 months.

FREEZER FRUIT

2 ripe, firm cantaloupe
1 watermelon
2 ripe, firm honeydew
1 cup sugar
1 quart water

. . . .

Wash fruit, cut in half lengthwise, and remove seeds. Scoop fruit into balls or cut into bite-size chunks. Dissolve sugar in water to make syrup. Place melon pieces in freezable container and cover with syrup. Allow headspace for expansion during freezing. Freeze up to 6 months. To serve: Allow to thaw at room temperature 30 minutes. Serve cold.

3 pounds fresh top sirloin steak
1/4 cup apple cider vinegar
2 tablespoons Worcestershire sauce
2 tablespoons olive oil
2 teaspoons garlic salt

Cut steak into serving pieces and place in freezer bag. In small bowl, combine remaining ingredients and add to bag with meat. Shake lightly to coat. Freeze up to 3 months. To serve: Thaw steak in bag with marinade. Grill and serve with vegetables and a salad. Do not reuse or serve marinade.

FESTIVE ICE CUBES

Oranges
Pineapple slices
Strawberries
Maraschino cherries
Cranberry juice cocktail

....

Slice fruit into small pieces, leaving the cherries
whole. Place fruit in ice cube trays. Cover fruit
pieces with cranberry juice cocktail. Freeze. Serve
in individual glasses or punch bowls.

Fresh broccoli

Wash broccoli well and divide into sprigs. Blanch
3 minutes in boiling water. Cool in ice water 3
minutes. Drain. Spread on wax paper-lined cookie
sheet in single layer. Cover with plastic wrap and
flash freeze by allowing broccoli to freeze for
about 30 minutes. Pack in freezer bags, remove air,
and freeze up to 6 months.

Fresh squash

....

Peel squash; cut it into pieces and cook in boiling water until almost tender. Drain and cool squash, and place in freezer bags. Remove air, seal, and store in freezer up to 3 months.

Always date and label your containers before you put them in the freezer. Label them with recipe name, date, number of servings, thawing and reheating directions, and "use-by" date. This will allow you to keep track of your stock as well as plan your weekly menus.

Quick
Tip

Fresh sweet potatoes

Cut sweet potatoes into pieces. Blanch 3 minutes in boiling water. Chill in ice water 2 to 3 minutes. Remove skin. Drain and place on cookie sheet in single layer. Flash freeze sweet potatoes by allowing them to freeze for about 30 minutes. Transfer to freezer bags and remove excess air. Freeze up to 6 months.

MORE FREEZABLES